Locating Europe

Empire And Nationalism In The Long Nineteenth Century

Gavin Murray-Miller

CHAPMAN MERRICK

Great Britain

First printing, 2016

Library of Congress Cataloging-in-Publication Data
Names: Murray-Miller, Gavin
Title: Locating Europe: Empire and Nationalism in
The Long Nineteenth Century
1. Europe—19th Century—History
2. Empire—19th Century—History
3. Nationalism—19th Century—History

Locating
Europe

In an entry for the massive *Encyclopédie* compiled during the middle of the eighteenth century, the French scholar Louis de Jaucourt, one of the most prolific contributors to the project, gave a concise definition of Europe which most educated readers of the period would have found familiar. Despite describing it as "the smallest part of the world," Jaucourt affirmed that Europe had "come to such a high degree of power that history has almost nothing on it." He noted the continent's debt to Christianity, a religion that had shaped European civilization's conception of "political right in government," respect for the "law of nations" and general "happiness." He equally underscored the innovative spirit that seemed to set Europe apart from other areas of the world. "It matters little that Europe is the smallest of the four parts of the world in terms of terrain," Jaucourt insisted, "because it is the largest of all with respect to its commerce, its navigation, its fertility, by the enlightenment and industry of its peoples, by the knowledge of Art, Science, [and] Trades."[1]

For Jaucourt, like many of his contemporaries, Europe was a qualifiable totality. It constituted a bounded geographic region united by specific traits and a shared historical development unique to the area and people. It had inherited common institutions from the Romans, furnishing an ancient foundation upon which Germanic traditions of kingship and law had been grafted over the centuries. This institutional framework was complemented by economic interdependence and a set of interests common to all from the Atlantic to the Eastern half of the continent. Overstating this semblance of unity, the *philosophe* Charles-Louis de Secondat, Baron de Montesquieu went as far as to remark: "Europe is a state made up of several provinces."[2] In spite of such exaggerations, it was difficult to deny that continental elites were coming to see themselves as part of a broader community. A shared classical inheritance, increasing diplomatic and commercial relations and a growing sense of Europe as both a place and civilization had come to outline what the British statesman Edmund Burke at the tail end of the eighteenth century would describe as "the great vicinage of Europe."[3]

"Europe" was by no means an alien concept to earlier generations. As early as 732, a medieval chronicler had referred to the people of the continent as *Europenses*. The term suggested a collectivity greater than the localized, kin-based Germanic kingdoms that had supplanted the Roman Empire on the continent, evoking memories of the lost *imperium romanum* that had once united the people of the region.[4] It was, therefore, not surprising that Charlemagne would adopt the title *pater europea*—"father of all Europeans"—in carving out his own continental empire during the late-eighth century. Throughout the Renaissance, the term had regularly been used, and indeed became synonymous with the variety of religious and ethnic groups populating the continent.[5] Yet "Europe" in the sense that it was employed by writers like Jaucourt and Burke was primarily an Enlightenment creation. The so-called "Grand Tour," a veritable tradition by the eighteenth century, acquainted elites with the marvels of a civilization they were coming to understand as properly "European." Young men gazed upon the ruins of Classical civilization in Italy and became versed in the refinements of modern civilization in Paris, partaking in an itinerant education that reinforced the cultural and historic commonalities bounding a continent. Through these travels, European civilization was not so much "discovered" as it was "invented" by those in search of it.[6]

The intellectual and cultural environment of the eighteenth century did much to foster continentalist perspectives. Writers and literati from across Europe participated in an extensive cosmopolitan exchange through correspondence networks and public debates spanning from London to Königsberg and St. Petersburg to Paris. Many *philosophes* prided themselves on their cosmopolitan credentials and engagement with a "republic of letters" consisting of Europe's most illustrious and notable personages. *Philosophes* were also peripatetic, whether out of personal curiosity or to avoid punishment incurred by their biting criticism of the political and religious institutions of the day. Forced to flee France in 1726 after a brusque retort invited the ire of an influential noble, Voltaire took up residence across the English Channel, relocated to Potsdam upon the invitation of Frederick II and temporarily settled in Geneva before returning to his native country. Thomas Paine left England for the shores of the North American colonies in 1774, found himself in France during the tumultuous 1790s and eventually died in New York in 1809. These migratory lifestyles were increasingly becoming common among Europe's new educated classes and even symbolized the essence of the new enlightened individual free of local prejudices and parochialism celebrated by *philosophes*.[7]

With their characteristic disdain for religious dogma and slavish obedience, the *philosophes* shared a rational and moral vision of man, emphasizing the capacity for intellectual refinement, politesse and morality. In particular, they lauded the social progress of the century evident in Europe's growing appreciation for international law, commerce and peaceful coexistence. It was precisely this sentiment that Emmanuel Kant expressed when alluding to "the civilized states of our continent, [and] especially the commercial states."[8] For Enlightenment thinkers, commerce and civilization worked together, promoting "order and good government, and with them, the liberty and security of individuals," as Adam Smith explained.[9] Accordingly, Europe's extensive trading networks and commercial enterprises bolstered a specific type of unity evident not only in mutual interests but in corresponding values and outlooks deemed "civilized." "The progress of commerce [has] considerable influence in polishing the manners of the European nations, and in leading them to order, equal laws and humanity," observed the Scottish philosopher William Roberts.[10] "Gentle commerce" (*doux commerce*), as Montesquieu phrased it, was the lynchpin of a Europe that, after a period of violent religious warfare and upheaval, was "no longer . . . one nation" yet nonetheless united in its sentiments and purpose.[11]

Praise for commerce was hardly unique to the eighteenth century. In the past, writers from the English theologian Richard Hooker to the Dutch jurist Hugo Grotius had defended the right of open waters and trade with allusions to the commonwealth of man and commerce's unifying potential.[12] Yet the perspicuous Eurocentric dimensions that Enlightenment thinkers attached to this process were relatively novel. Gentle commerce, accompanied by its handmaidens liberty and progress, were the conquests of Europe proper, a conviction that emphasized an understanding of Europe's special role and place in the larger world.[13] More specific, this superiority derived from the particular style of governance and public authority partial to the continent and its antique patrimony: civil society.[14] In the opinions of leading political philosophers, it was through the development of civil discourse and sociability that the benefits of liberty were actualized, that commercial success and productivity were promoted and man's perfection attained. If man began in a state of "rudeness" and savagery, civil society polished him and led the way from "barbarism to refinement," as Adam Ferguson remarked in the introduction to his *Essay on the History of Civil Society*.[15]

While the attributes of civilization were claimed as European, they were not exclusively so. The French economist and statesman Anne Robert Jacques Turgot expressed a widely held Enlightenment belief when arguing that the human race was "one vast whole" but that "the present state of the world, marked as it is by infinite variations in inequality spreads out before us at one and the same time all the gradations of barbarism to refinement."[16] Turgot and his contemporaries exhibited a tendency to think comparatively, often arriving at their theories on natural law, government and social institutions in relation to the disparities or "varieties" found in human societies.[17] "Varieties are but steps in the history of mankind," explained Adam Ferguson. They were indicative of "the fleeting and transient situation" through which all societies passed.[18] Enlightenment universalism may have conceptualized a civilizing process at work in world history, but it was clearly one in which Europe was leading the way. From this position, it did not take a stretch of the imagination to believe that Europe, with its global trading networks and imperial domains, could serve as an agent of civilization in the world. "What have been no better than the counting-houses of brigands will become colonies of citizens propagating throughout Africa and Asia the principles and the practice of liberty, knowledge and reason that they have brought from Europe," the Marquis de Condorcet prophesized.[19] By the end of the eighteenth century, reverence for *doux commerce* and its salubrious influences had been converted into a paternalistic civilizing mission anchored in the certainty of Europe's world preeminence.

Condorcet wrote in the midst of the French Revolution, an event that would radically redefine life and attitudes on the continent within the short span of two decades. Inspired by ideals of patriotism and universal liberty, radical revolutionaries in France transformed their national revolution into a European crusade. France, they claimed, was engaged in a common struggle against monarchy and committed to liberating the oppressed peoples of the continent. The irenic dream of a "republic of commerce" was eclipsed by a new era of apocalyptic oratory and nationalist zealotry. Yet if the French Revolution and subsequent Napoleonic Wars effectively shattered the European peace, they did not undermine faith in the essential idea of a shared European inheritance or worldview. On the contrary, belief in European unity was fortified during the years of revolutionary upheaval. The territorial expansion and universalist rhetoric of the Revolution saw the extension of French military power and personnel across the continent, and with these came French ideas and institutions. Crossing the Rhine and Alps, French forces assisted with the creation of national "sister republics" from Italy to the Balkans in the spirit of fraternal "reunion."

Within a decade, this style of republican nation-building was reconfigured into an ambitious vision of French continental hegemony as Napoleon Bonaparte took the reins of power. The patchwork of principalities and kingdoms scattered across the central and eastern portions of the continent were remodeled and incorporated into a European confederation under French aegis. Europe was integrated like never before with modern administrative bodies, uniform systems of measurement, a common legal framework (the Code Napoléon) and military bureaucracies. Underpinning this institutional homogenization was a common ideological struggle of national independence and liberty as newly-minted citizens were instructed to take up arms and fight alongside their French liberators. Whether espousing revolutionary values out of political conviction or merely collaborating with the invading French forces for opportunistic reasons, Europeans were conscious of participating in a continent-wide experience.[20] Napoleon himself bolstered such perceptions, tactfully crafting his legacy within the context of European unity and reform. Reflecting on his achievements *ex post facto* from exile in dreary Saint Helena, the former French Emperor confessed to his memorialist, "I [wished] to found a European system, a European Code of Laws, a European judiciary [so that] there would be but one people in Europe."[21]

It was, however, more than just institutions that the Napoleonic legacy bequeathed to the continent. In the wake of revolution and military expansion, a particular idea of Europe had solidified. Wherever French forces planted their flag they brought "civilization," a term synonymous with Europe and, ultimately, the French nation itself. Napoleonic administrators dispatched to the eastern periphery repeatedly commented on the backward and barbaric populations they encountered in these regions. "It is surprising to find such barbarism in the midst of European civilization," one official reported from Dalmatia in 1813, remarking on the evident differences between France and Europe's wild hinterland.[22] Creating a European people meant creating a civilized people, and French reforms never masked their intent to implant a uniform and superior culture within conquered territories. Under Napoleon, Europe effectively became "Europeanized."

By the end of the Napoleonic Wars, Enlightenment perspectives on commerce and moral progress had crystalized into a comprehensive vision of Europe not only as a continental community but as a world-historical phenomenon. The years of revolutionary turmoil born from 1789 had provided the final impetus in this development. "After having shattered, ruptured and demolished everything it had been, is [the continent] not completely occupied with finding itself, remaking itself and recreating itself?" asked the French political writer Émile Barrault in 1835. Violently torn asunder from its Christian and monarchial heritage, the people of the

11

continent were now encouraged to reimagine themselves as part of a civilization that, in Barrault's estimation, designated "something immense, incomplete, prolific, confusing, [and] new . . . something that embraces everything and yet still has no clearly defined form; a chaos pregnant with creation yet inchoate."[23] The restless energies of the late-eighteenth century had found expression in Enlightenment notions of civility, social progress and the republic of commerce. The revolutionary fury they unleashed, however, was a different animal. The Revolution marked a dramatic rupture with the past, a violent act of self-repudiation and renewal. "Europe" gave embodiment and symbolic form to this process; to its destructive and creative impulses, to its moral élan and universalism, to the *terra incognita* of modernity.

"There exists in Europe a concord of needs and wishes, a common thought, a universal soul, that drives nations toward the same goal," the Italian nationalist Giuseppe Mazzini affirmed in 1831. "There exists a European tendency."[24] Yet what was this tendency? For political ideologues like Mazzini it signified the promise of liberty, the union of people and, above all, peace. For technocratic thinkers like Barrault, Europe pointed the way to humanity's future as the driving force of an unprecedented industrial and commercial world order. These moral and progressive affinities constituted the basis of a European idea that future generations would repeatedly invoke and identify with over the coming years. By 1867, the philosopher Émile Littré could speak of Europe as an "innate tendency."

The people of the continent, he insisted, now "truly feel like citizens of that vast and glorious community we call Europe."[25]

If the idiom of Europe was obtaining wider currency in defining a certain idea of community, geographically locating Europe proved more difficult. Increased travel and knowledge of the continent ironically resulted in greater ambiguity over Europe's exact coordinates. As early as the sixteenth century, cartographers and surveyors had provided audiences with physicals representations of Europe charting the expanse of the continent. Maps detailed a wide swath of territory stretching from the Mediterranean to the Baltic and from the Atlantic coast to the Turkish borderlands in the east, all of which encompassed a rough geographic expanse imagined as Europe.[26] During the mid-1700s, the Russian polymath and cartographer Vasilii Tatishchev saw fit to set the boundary line of continental Europe and Asia at the Ural Mountains, conspicuously including the western Slavic portion of his native Russia within the geography of Europe.[27] Having spent his career in the Urals region overseeing mining operations and taming the Bashkir people of the steppe, Tatishchev was inclined to draw distinctions between the Slavic populations to the West and the "savages" inhabiting Tatarstan. His border drawing equally pleased his ruler and patron Tsar Peter the Great, who intended to promote an image of Russia as a "civilized" Europe power rather than an Asiatic backwater. His newly-built capital of St. Petersburg located on the Baltic coast was to serve as a "window on the west," and this could only be the case if Russia itself was placed within Europe.[28] Under the circumstances, Tatishchev was free to take certain liberties in his cartographic enterprise.

This was not to imply that Tatishchev's Europeanization of western Russia was accepted as fact. When the diplomat Louis-Philippe de Ségur was dispatched to attend Catherine the Great's jubilee in 1787, the French count was inclined to believe otherwise. Celebrating twenty-five years on the throne, the Tsarina decided to show off her newly acquired Black Sea territory and staged the scheduled festivities in the Crimea. German-born and French-educated, Catherine was an admirer of Peter's westernizing initiatives and had seen through a series of her own westernizing reforms as well. Her law code promulgated in 1767—the *Nakaz*—left no question as to her outlook, stridently declaring "Russia is a European power."[29] Yet Ségur remained skeptical as to whether Russia in fact lay within Europe. Crossing the border between Prussia and Poland, he glimpsed a dismal landscape from his carriage window of impoverished people and squalid villages with "cottages little different from savage huts." "Everything makes you think you have gone back ten centuries, finding yourself amid hordes of Huns, Scythians, Veneti, Slavs and Sarmatians," he wrote contemptuously. In his verdict, "When one enters Poland, they believe themselves to have left Europe entirely."[30] Russians themselves did not always put stock in

this imaginative geography. For the journalist and war correspondent Vsevolod Vladimirovich Krestosvskii, the Danube constituted
the frontier of Europe and Asia. Stationed in Bulgaria during the
Eastern Crisis of 1878, he would look across the banks of the river
to neighboring Romania, remarking, "There is Europe and here
Asia."[31]

The boundaries of Europe were often murky beyond the
Prussian heartland in the north and the frontier of the Habsburg
Empire to the south-east, creating a labile middle ground that was
open to interpretation. Traditional views conceptualized a north-
south continental division distinguishing between the Latinized
Mediterranean regions of the former Roman Empire and a largely
Germanic north. Beginning in the eighteenth century, however, perspectives shifted. Europe was re-mapped along an east-west axis,
with "Oriental Europe" increasingly relegated to the fringes of the
continent both spatially and culturally.[32] What the Greeks and Romans had formerly categorized as Europa—territories including
Thrace, Macedonia, Illyria and portions of Bulgaria—was by the
nineteenth century considered only marginally European at best. On
his trek through the Balkans in the early-twentieth century, the British travel writer and explorer Harry de Windt referred to the area as
"Savage Europe," depicting it as a wild frontier region similar to the
American West.[33] He was hardly alone in this assessment. The Aus-
trian statesman Klemens von Metternich fixed the European frontier significantly further west. "Asia begins at the Landstrasse," he

famously quipped, designating the royal highway leading out of Vienna as the boundary separating East and West.[34] To the west, boundaries could be just as fluid. Visiting Spain in the early 1840s, the French travel writer Théophile Gautier was enchanted by the Oriental qualities and exoticism he found. "Spain . . . is not made for European mores," he wrote. "The genius of the Orient reveals itself under all forms here."[35]

East and West, Asia and Europe "were always walls in the mind at least as much as lines on the earth," as the historian Tony Judt once claimed.[36] As such, these toponyms could be expansive or restrictive. As a geographical expression, Europe possessed a form that was roughly identifiable. Yet as a concept, its contours could be limitless. This was especially true as Europeans began to settle in other parts of the world during the nineteenth century. In an age that witnessed the rise of global empires, Europe itself acquired a global character.

———

In January of 1859, William Howard Russell arrived at Galle, a port city located on the tip of Sri Lanka. An Irish correspondent for *The Times*, Russell had been sent to subcontinental Asia to report on the situation following the 1857 Sepoy Rebellion, a considerable native uprising that had momentarily threatened British power in India. Galle had been a Dutch garrison before being transferred to British control in the late-eighteenth century as the East India Company consolidated its hold over India. Upon landing, Russell took up lodging at a hotel occupied by guests from China, Australia and Indonesia. Most came for business, and the streets of Galle attested to the island's lively economy. Merchants hawked cheap Chinese parasols. Market stalls were stacked with ivory paper weights and elaborately carved boxes. Vendors enticed customers with displays of emeralds and diamonds which, Russell noted cynically, were imitations hardly worth their asking price. Despite more than sixty years of British control, the former Dutch presence was evident throughout the city. The buildings were all done in old European style with the type of high gabled roofs and iron gateways that had since disappeared on the continent. "Galle . . . is the oldest place in the world. Here is a slice of old Europe, 200 years old, thrust in among the cocoanut tress, palms, coral reefs . . .," he wrote.[37] The surreal element of this discovery was not lost on Russell. He had traveled over 5,000 miles only to find himself transported back in time to "old Europe" on the coast of Asia.

Galle was by no means exceptional. Many European travelers had similar experiences of departing from their native land to find themselves surrounded by reminders of the Europe they had left. Since the sixteenth century, European powers had been busy carving out vast global empires, and the effects of this empire-building were discernible in the various colonial settlements and protectorates scattered throughout the world.

In the early 1870s, the Scottish missionary Norman Macleod arrived in Bombay on the Western coast of mainland Indian to find a "Europeanised city" bustling with commerce and trade.[38] The cotton boom of the 1860s had been instrumental in transforming this former garrison town ruled by the East India Company into a colonial urban metropolis supervised directly by a technocratic and well-oiled imperial administration. With the American Civil War disrupting cotton imports across the Atlantic, Bombay quickly became the chief hub of Britain's colonial cotton industry. Infrastructure and transport were developed to facilitate shipping, mills built to process raw cotton and structures erected in accordance with the tastes of the city's new merchant class rising to predominance. The central Esplanade featured lines of edifices done up in gothic Victorian style while Bombay University, established in 1857 at the behest of the British Bombay Association, similarly testified to Britain's growing presence on the subcontinent. Modeled on the University of London, its imposing buildings and gothic clock tower were redolent of the British Isles and suggestive of Britain's "civilizing" influence in Asia. Yet "the jewel" of British Bombay was the grand Victoria Terminus built to headquarter the Great Indian Peninsular Railway in 1887. Based on London's St. Pancras rail station, the central rail terminal was intended as a tribute to British ingenuity and commerce in the nineteenth century, marking Bombay as a rapidly industrializing city akin to London, Manchester or Liverpool. These monuments of colonial grandeur were only the most remarkable examples of the mark left by Britain on the city. Writing at the end of the nineteenth century, James Furneaux, editor for the *Times of India*, summed up the impression that many Europeans held upon arriving, insisting that the Yacht Club, the imposing arcades of the Apollo Restaurant and the electric lights all reminded him of his native land.[39]

Much the same could be said regarding other subcontinental cities. In Calcutta, it was difficult to ignore the resemblance between the stately St. Andrew's Kirk and London's own St. Martin-in-the-Fields. Those who had grown rich from imperial trade in muslin, indigo and spices built palatial homes while the East India Company oversaw the construction of wide avenues, squares and commercial centers in the "white town" district inhabited primarily by Europeans. The seat of the East India Company, the Writers' Building, sported a handsome portico with ionic columns and parapets adorned with Greco-Roman statues and thronged by palm trees. Much as in Bombay, industry had transfigured the Bengali capital, outfitting it with docks and factories along the waterfront. With British industry also came the miseries of industrialization. The thick smoke that hung in the air and the teams of poor laborers milling about the wharfs easily brought to mind the unseemlier aspects of the industrial revolution evident back home in the British Isles. "Why this is London!" Rudyard Kipling mocked when describing the quayside around Hughli Bridge in 1891. "This is the docks. This in Imperial. This is worth coming across India to see!"[40]

While the parallels between European cities and their colonial counterparts could be exaggerated, the similarities found in the colonies did hint at a common experience to which many observers were sensitive. The nineteenth century constituted a period of significant economic modernization and urbanization in European capitals. The construction of railways and palatial neo-gothic buildings in Bombay was coterminous with similar feats back home as new building projects and the laying of the London Underground proceeded alongside the growth of urban slums in neighborhoods like Whapping and the East End. Taking a trip down the Thames in 1877, Henry James commented on the pollution, "dead-faced warehouses and frowsy people," stating, "all this smudgy detail may remind you of nothing less than the wealth and power of the British Empire at large."[41] Imperial expansion certainly played a role in Britain's industrial prowess. Yet the relationship between the British metropole and its colonies extended far beyond the obvious links of commerce and trade. What James witnessed from a steamboat on the Thames, Kipling similarly found on the banks of the Hughli in Bengal. Moreover, the scope and transformative nature of the public works projects being carried out in places like Bombay could have equally applied to any number of European cities at this time. By the 1870s, Vienna was in the midst of a substantial modernizing program evident in the tramlines and *Prachtbauen* of the Ringstrasse that would fuel the birth of Viennese urban modernism.[42] By the end of century, Baron Frigyes Podmaniczky would follow suit in the

Habsburg Empire's second capital. Committed to portraying Hungary as a modern power, Podmaniczky recreated Budapest in the image of a progressive urban capital with expansive boulevards like Andrássy Avenue, a gothic-revival parliament situated on the Danube waterfront and the continent's first underground metro system. Nineteenth-century European urbanization correlated with comparable initiatives in cities such as Calcutta and Bombay as public works projects grappled with problems of providing residents with utilities and amenities, combating urban diseases through public hygiene, accommodating the needs of industrial production and reconciling new wealth with stark displays of urban squalor.

The model *par excellence* for many of these urbanizing initiatives was Paris. Under Emperor Napoleon III and his ambitious prefect Baron Georges Haussmann, the French capital became the archetype of the new urban metropolis. Old medieval sections of the city were readily demolished and replaced by apartment buildings and restaurants catering to upscale bourgeois residents. Public gardens and boulevards lined with department stores bisected and blotted out former working class districts to facilitated trade and precluded the types of working-class protests that had notoriously roiled the city in the past. Yet like Britain, France was also in possession of a vast overseas colonial empire, and the urbanization taking place at home mirrored efforts at empire-building abroad. In 1830, France launched an invasion of Ottoman Algiers, effectively seizing the Mediterranean city and setting in motion a new round of colonial expansion that would place large swaths of North Africa under French control by the end of the century. As Haussmann was busy remodeling Paris during the 1850s and 1860s, Algiers was subject to its own modernizing process under the civil engineer Charles Frédéric Chassériau. Outlining the project, Prince Jérôme Napoleon enumerated the state's desire for esplanades, docks, attractive buildings and national monuments: "in a word, everything that can strike the imagination, be useful and give a grand idea of France and the Emperor." The city was intended to give a great deal of "prestige" to the government, as he saw it.[43] To this end, expansive boulevards—like the Boulevard de l'Impératrice with its sprawling neo-classical promenade—were constructed along the waterfront. Areas surrounding the Arab Casbah quarter were outfitted with broad streets, shopping districts and *haussmannisé*-inspired buildings. As France consolidated it hold on Algiers, a new European city spread out around the old city center and along the coast.[44] Appraising the work in 1852, the Orientalist painter Eugène Fromentin balked at the new landscape of "Parisian imitations" that was quickly eclipsing the native Moorish architecture.[45]

Visitors coming from Paris or Marseille found all the amenities and vices that their home cities had to offer. Yet the *presence française* not only imparted a more European character to Algeria; it also brought more Europeans to North Africa *tout court* as colonists, merchants and tourists traveled across the Mediterranean in unprecedented numbers.[46] It was not uncommon to find Europeans sitting at cafés reading French newspapers and sipping absinthe in France's new colonial capital. At night, cabarets, casinos and brothels provided cheap entertainment while more upscale visitors and residents amused themselves with musical performances and plays put on at the theaters and music halls. Already by the 1840s, hotels like those run by Latour-Dupin had been erected in central Algiers to cater to European tourism. As one observer described it, Latour-Dupin's establishment was "very beautiful and built in French, or rather Parisian, style with large windows and arcades made to resemble those of the rue du Rivoli."[47] With its hotels, *grands magasins* and growing European population, comparison with Paris was not unthinkable, and many French commentators saw fit to stress such similarities. Inspired by a new sense of colonial mission, French critics hailed Algeria as a "new France" or "southern *département*" while the Mediterranean was considered nothing more than a "French lake." This was precisely the impression the dignitary Albert de Broglie had during his visit to Algiers in the late 1850s. "[In the evenings] the Moorish women appear on their terraces to enjoy the sea breeze while below their feet the European constructions of the lower city are reflected in the still waters of the port . . . . Yesterday it was the desert. Today it is France!"[48] Much as Prince Napoleon had anticipated, Algiers was envisioned as a monument to French imperial grandeur and national prestige, a Paris on the shores of savage Africa. In the words of one journalist, France had taken an Oriental city and made it into a modern one, "heroically implanting [its civilization] in the heart of barbarism."[49]

Such pretensions fueled overseas building projects as the nineteenth century progressed. Yet colonial regimes were not simply engaged in transplanting and copying European forms on distant shores, despite the pronouncements of imperial ideologues and statesmen to this effect. Replicating Europe on foreign continents marked conscious efforts to create a specific idea and image of Europe, a "simulacra" that was always more symbolic than authentic.[50] Claims to civilizing and modernizing non-European territories furnished the ideological fiction and rationale of imperial expansion and conquest. As such, Europe, civilization and modernity became intermingled concepts, with one commonly serving as a metonym for the other. In projecting images of themselves as "modern" societies, states and rulers employed a symbolism and vocabulary broadly understood to be European, and in doing so validated their status as nominally modern, civilized nations. This was especially important for states with only marginal European credentials or regions considered altogether "Oriental" and foreign.[51] In these instances, Europeanization occurred by design as much as by tendency, demonstrating the malleability and competitive impulses that motivated nineteenth-century urbanizations initiatives on a global scale.

Case in point was Russia. Straddling the boundaries between Europe and Asia, the Russian Empire perennially tested the limits of European inclusion and exclusion. Its entrenched feudal hierarchies and religious culture were reminiscent of Europe's bygone medieval age while its traditions of autocratic rule reflected the "despotism" familiar to Oriental societies. A predominantly agrarian economy worked by a landed serf class inhibited the industrial development and capitalist entrepreneurship ascendant in the West. Religious mysticism and a strong devotion to Orthodox liturgy proved resistant to enlightened ideas just as its multi-ethnic populace appeared incompatible with the model of the continental nation-state. These and other aspects of Russian society set the Tsarist regime apart from the West and typically frustrated reform-minded Tsars seeking consideration as proper European monarchs. Whereas Peter the Great had intended the Western-styled city of St. Petersburg to symbolize Russia's status as a great European power in the 1700s, in the following century officials set their sights on the newly conquered territories in Central Asia.

In particular, the colony of Turkestan formally created in 1867 provided a new opportunity to recreate Russia in the image of the West. The military governor of Turkestan, Konstantin von Kaufman, was not reticent when it came to his goals of spreading enlightenment and civilization among the Muslim populations of the region. His policies aimed at demonstrating the benefits of Russian civilization, a task equated with combatting the religious fanaticism and backwardness of the natives through good administration and the promotion of scientific knowledge. To achieve this end, Kaufman employed a team of engineers and scholars and pressed them into the service of Russian empire-building. The painter Vasilii

Vereshchagin was commissioned by the military administration at the start of the expedition to record the ethnic groups of Central Asia and provide the administration with much needed information on the local peoples of the region.[52] His work was equally useful in depicting acts of Russian heroism and "civilization" in action. Exhibited at London's Crystal Palace in 1873, Vereshchagin's canvases were used to publicize Russia's new colonial mission to an international audience. The preface to the exhibition catalogue expressed the government's public relations objectives in no uncertain terms: "The Central Asian population's barbarism is so glaring, its economic and social condition so degraded, that the sooner European civilization penetrates into the land, whether from one side or the other, the better."[53] Without question, it was Russia delivering the benefits of this supposed "European" civilization, affirming Russia's place among the leading colonial powers of the world.

At the center of this colonial braggadocio stood Tashkent, the Turkic trading hub envisaged as the capital of Russia's new colony. The Russian-born Swiss explorer Henri Morse had come to Tashkent in 1869 at the early stages of the Russian occupation, finding a sad village with dusty streets and mud huts situated in the middle of the abyss that was the Central Asian steppe. Returning in 1882, he encountered a "lovely and pleasant" city complete with wide streets, canals and buildings similar to "any number of Europe's cities." To his astonishment there was even a theater that staged performances similar to those put on at the Paris Opera

House. "Russian Tashkent has the genuine look of a small European capital," he claimed.[54] In colonial Tashkent, balls and concerts were put on for settlers and officials while people could spend their days in the local social clubs lazily reading newspapers or playing billiards.[55] Within the span of twenty years, the Russian colonial administration and its team of civil engineers managed to outfit the city with boulevards and poplar-lined streets modeled on St. Petersburg's Nevskii Prospect. These Russian elements were complemented by a Parisian-inspired network of streets, parks shaded by apricot trees and a public zoo that gave Tashkent's new "European quarter" a distinct charm and character of its own.

Tashkent was lauded as an oasis of European civilization in the middle of Central Asia, an impression that the Russian administration assiduously cultivated as it carried out its work.[56] If Russia's European and civilized pedigree may have been questionable among French and British observers, its robust efforts to civilize the steppe and impart a "European" character to the region amounted to an exercise in radical self-fashioning. "In Europe we were Tatars," wrote Fyodor Dostoyevsky in 1881, "but in Asia we were also Europeans."[57] Colonialism provided an important theater in which Russian identity could be manufactured and projected to the rest of the world. The official newspaper *Turkestanskiia Viedomosti* spelled out these intentions clearly in its inaugural issue, noting, "Turkestan can be as important for us as India is for Britain and Algeria for France."[58] The comparison was apt.[59] Colonial cities like Algiers,

Bombay and Tashkent provided stages upon which the drama of European modernity and progress was played out and represented to audiences at home and abroad. They were testaments to European power, but equally symbols that were consciously constructed and molded to communicate notions of European civilization and self-hood. The Spanish politician and economist Joaquín Costa revealed the power such mentalities exercised on the imagination when calling upon his native country to bring civilization to its Moroccan territories in 1884. Spain should "reproduce down there the character of our homeland" and created an "African Spain" in the image of the metro-pole, Costa urged his compatriots.[60]

In both its ideology and practice, colonialism continually ex-pressed a desire to reproduce Europe culturally, socially and topo-graphically upon distant shores. It implanted and attempted to naturalize European populations on faraway continents, introduced new cultural values and endowed regions with new toponyms and identities. In the process, Europe was transformed from a geographic reference into an idea, one that proved exceedingly malleable and cap-able of taking root in almost any soil.

And it was not simply colonial European powers that engaged in this type of artful self-fashioning either. As nominally European at-tributes became benchmarks of civility and progress, non-Western powers also learned to speak the language of "civilization" and "en-lightenment" espoused by imperial rivals. Forward-looking emirs or sultans under pressure from foreign powers were attracted to the financial and military benefits that reforms might offer. For more than a century, the Ottoman leadership walked a fine line between modernization and tradition, contending with the needs of state reform while catering to religious conservatives and wary elites within the military.[61] Although this balancing act did not always proceed smoothly, the expanding influence of European power in Ottoman economic affairs and the strains of imperial decline made it a necessity. "Constantinople looks a lot like London and nothing like the Orient," Gautier wrote back to a friend, unamused, following a trip to the city in the 1850s.[62]

As in Istanbul, so too in Egypt. Alexandria's cosmopolitan atmosphere, European buildings and modern train stations evoked nothing of the city's classical heritage, while Cairo had little of the "authentic" Orient to offer the tourist. Docking in the city on his way to India, William Howard Russell took a critical view of Cairo, a city "most distressingly European" in its look and character. "Tall gaunt French and Italian looking houses seem staring at each other over partitions and garden walls as if in surprise at finding themselves in such a place," he wrote in 1858. "The junction between the two is as ill-assorted as a Paisley fringe to a Cashmere shawl."[63] Just over a decade later, the contrast was even more glaring. The French-educated and reform-minded Khedive Ismāʿīl Pāshā successfully oversaw an ambitious project of modernization with the intention of rapprochement with the European powers. During the 1860s, Ismāʿīl Pāshā had made it a point to advertise his policies in the capitals of Europe, often using international exhibitions and trade fairs to publicize the "new" Egypt. In 1869, he crowned his achievements with the opening of the Suez Canal, an event that drew international attention and praise from European commentators who waxed lyrical on the progressive changes taking place in the country. In anticipation of the European guests set to attend the inauguration ceremonies, Cairo was given a European facelift with papers touting the city as "the Paris of the Orient."[64] European music was heard emanating from cafés and restaurants while the Place de l'Ezbekieh teemed with crowds of European tourists attending performances at the newly-constructed Théâtre du Cirque and Comédie-Française. "Without the distinguishable minarets and palm trees you would hardly believe yourself to be in Africa," remarked Gautier.[65] This impression was precisely what the ambitious Khedive had envisioned in the early 1860s, and he was not modest when it came to touting his accomplishments. "My country is no longer in Africa," he proclaimed resolutely in 1878. "We are now part of Europe."[66]

Even the Far East was not immune to such transformations. Prior to the 1850s, Japan's tradition of isolationism had shielded the island from foreign and "barbaric" influences. Yet with the opening of Japanese ports to foreign merchants beginning in the 1860s, a generation of Japanese statesmen and intellectuals embraced westernization as the guiding mantra of a "new Japan." Elegant kimonos gave way to high-collared shirts and overcoats; the matted floors and lacquered writing tables traditionally found in offices and trade agencies were replaced with desks and chairs imported from Europe. According to Sir David Wedderburn who undertook an extensive voyage across Asia and the Pacific in the 1870s, the Victorian public now only asked a single question when it came to the land of the rising sun: "Will not the distinctive charms of Japanese life and manners within a few years disappear forever beneath the monotonous surface of modern civilization?"[67] Assessing the newly-laid rail lines—a potent symbol of modernization in the nineteenth century—commissioned by the state in the decade after the Meiji restoration, the British naval commander of the Pacific fleet, Cyprian Bridge, saw these innovations as nothing short of grotesque, denouncing them as the "ugly scar of 'Western Progress'—the shibboleth of New Japan."[68] In his opinion, the railroad was only one of many foreign influences perverting the beauty and traditions of "the real Japan." He execrated everything from the "copies of European restaurants" beginning to replace Kyoto tea-houses to the arrival of Christian missionaries and the seemingly insatiable infatuation for all things western currently in vogue among Japanese elites. "It is a pitiful tale, this overwhelming of an interesting and even romantic country by a deluge of vulgar common-place," Bridge despaired. "Those who would see anything of the real Japan should visit the country without delay."[69]

Bridge was not alone in his appraisal of the conspicuous Western influences growing up in foreign societies. When it came to

Cairo and Damascus, the British journalist and Orientalist Ellis Schaap contended that European luxuries and amenities had not only corrupted these cities, but effectively "de-Orientalized" them. "The presence of countless trippers in sober Occidental garb, of motors and carriages, to say nothing of French cafés and cinema shows, and the bandying words in English, French, Greek and Italian, leaves an unpleasant impression upon the mind of an inharmonious whole, neither true East nor true West."[70] What Japanese and Egyptians thought of as novel and innovative, many Europeans criticized as vulgar and commonplace, seeing in these changes only a threat to "old Japan" or the "old Orient" with its rich traditions, style and patently Oriental traits. Yet these visions of Oriental life and society had always been more European fantasy than reality, an Orient culled from romantic travel accounts, salon paintings and opera performances rather than actual experience or accurate knowledge. Travelers seeking out the exotic and picturesque were bound to be disappointed, finding European "imitations" and colonial hybrids instead of "authentic" Oriental cities. As William Howard Russell rhetorically asked when observing the landscape of Bengal in 1858: "Where are the glories of the gorgeous east in scenery, clouds, skies, jewels, purple or fine linen palaces? I see them not."[71]

"Now is the time to see the Orient because it's disappearing, it's getting civilized," Gustave Flaubert advised his mother in a letter written during a trip through Egypt and the Levant in the late 1840s.[72] Of course what he meant by this comment was that the

East resembled Europe to a greater extent than he had previously imagined, and in this assessment he was not alone. The playwright Ernest Feydeau expressed his discontent with colonial Algiers in a long lament to modernity's degrading and homogenizing influences, imaging a future in which every point on the globe would be identical and everyone free to live a life of sheer boredom. This sterile mediocrity was foreshadowed by the new Paris growing up on the African coast. "The Orient is disappearing," he mourned while gazing upon the landscape of boulevards and Turks drinking at French cafés. "It is disputing the terrain step by step, but it is disappearing with its exquisite forms."[73] A half-century later Charles Rosher, a onetime British resident artist in Morocco who turned to journalism later in life, gave a similarly bleak assessment of Tangiers under French rule. "It has already been spoilt, and with a sigh of regret for the picturesque past we must recognize *le fait accompli*, and put up with hideous examples of modernity in architecture, and expect to see a new Tangier spreading itself out round the blue waters of the bay dominated perhaps by a new Monte Carlo on Tebel Charf."[74]

These elegies to the exoticism and charm of a fabled Orient were in part the product of an aggressive European colonialism and in part a reaction to a globalized modernizing process taking place across the nineteenth century. If Europeans left home to find only the simulacra of Paris or London, their experiences testified to modernity's pervasive influences just as much as to Europe's increasing global reach and prestige.

The new European vistas that took shape abroad were characterized by evident tension between the native and the foreign. Bridge's lament for "old Japan" or Feydeau's longing for a mythic Orient may have been products of a maudlin nostalgia for an imaginary pre-modern paradise. Nevertheless, they did underscore certain realities of the colonial encounter that were difficult to ignore. Fromentin, perennially resentful of colonial modernization, criticized the trans-formations that came with a Gallicized Algiers. "Proceeding by the principle of tabula rasa, civilization has begun by tearing down everything not in accordance with its tastes," he remarked.[75] The street bazaars had disappeared along with the Arabs who had once attended them. Whole sections of the city lay in ruin. The native population found itself relegated to the Casbah district or pushed to surrounding regions of the city, compelled to make room for the arriving European colonists. "Today Algiers is an entirely European city," the traveling businessman Charles Thierry-Mieg stated in 1860. "The Arabs that one sees there already seem so completely exiled that it is popularly said they now only serve as ornaments for the landscape and to remind people that Algiers was not always a French city."[76]

Although hyperbolic, Thierry-Mieg's pronouncement did under-score a critical difference of "new France" when compared with Calcutta or Bombay. Unlike British India which had been largely conquered and settled by a mercantile trading firm, Algeria was intended to be a settler colony almost from the very beginning. By its very nature, the European presence in North Africa was significantly more pronounced as the colonial administration attempted to accommodate an incoming population "dreaming of Alsace and Normandy under the palm trees," as Feydeau quipped.[77] In itself, this strategy implied a different rationale in urban planning and administration. It was not only European architecture and enterprises that were being exported to the colonies, but people. Land was needed for settlement, and in most cases this unquestionably came at the expense and displacement of the indigenous peoples. In 1842, the abbot Eustache-Alexander Carron had passed through the city of Blida, a mere fifty kilometers outside Algiers, where he found a "Moorish" city. Returning two years later, he found that "a French city had taken the place of the Arab one."[78] This occurrence would increasingly become more common as European settlement took root not only in North Africa but across the globe.

Throughout the nineteenth century, Europeans moved across the world and settled on distant shores at a rate that was previously unknown. As imperial competition revved up during the late-eighteenth and early-nineteenth centuries, states began taking more active and direct roles in administering their overseas territories. Populating colonies with loyal and hardworking citizens offered one means of developing land and consolidating a strong imperial presence in regions with relatively thin populations of European traders and merchants. In addition to supplanting hostile natives with European laborers and consumers, settler colonialism also held the potential benefit of acting as a safety valve for mounting domestic pressures caused by population growth and industrialization. As land short-ages and unemployment generated social unrest on the continent, colonies were increasingly envisioned as convenient spaces to un-load surplus labor and undesirables.

These objectives were clearly laid out in the 1820s by the Lon-don Emigration Committee, a body committed to domestic and co-lonial reform in Great Britain. Edmund Gibbons Wakefield, a chief spokesman for the group, earned a reputation as an enthusiastic supporter of British colonial expansion in the South Pacific, arguing for a government-sponsored program of emigration and resettle-ment in Australia to remedy the social ills afflicting the nation. In a series of books and pamphlets, Wakefield reasoned that systematic colonization would reduce social competition at home and eliminate the threat of social revolution that constantly loomed over British society.[79] What was required was a concerted effort on the part of the state to encourage settlement abroad and provide conditions fa-vorable for emigration. After years of consistent lobbying efforts, the scheme was adopted in 1834. The government agreed to provide free transport and cheap land for anybody willing to make the trip to South Australia. By 1850, some 125,000 settlers had taken up the offer, with British subjects migrating to Australia and New South Wales at the behest of the metropolitan government.[80]

A similar turn of events transpired in France. After 1830, the French government undertook a propaganda campaign to draw settlers to Algeria. It offered concessions and transport for competent agricultural workers and even employed pamphlet writers to advertise the region and make it attractive to prospective colonists.[81] Between 1848 and 1852—a period marked by extreme political and economic turmoil on the continent—French authorities enacted more aggressive policies. Following a failed social revolution that traumatized the country in 1848, unemployed workers and political dissidents were exported to Algeria by the thousands. The deputy Jacques-Charles Brunet did not mince words, stating, "the colonization of Algeria is one of the most effective means at present of coming to improve misery [in our country]."[82] Fears regarding demographic growth in the countryside and the threat idle workers posed to social order encouraged support for the measure, with some 12,000 French citizens transported to Algeria over the next three years. The plan provided a politically expedient means of supporting colonization and putting an end to domestic social turmoil in one stroke.[83]

Labor militancy (or the fear of it) was not the only motivating factor behind colonial resettlement policies. In 1830, Tsar Nicholas I authorized the relocation of "pernicious" religious sects to Transcaucasia with the intention of segregating dissenting groups like the Dukhobars and Subbotniks from the Orthodox Christian population. While the decree was driven by desires to resolve internal religious tensions within the empire, the plan furthered Russian expansion in the south and served to populate the imperial frontier, resulting in a form of "accidental" colonization that sustained a Russian presence in the borderlands.[84] Russian settlement across Central Asia, European emigration throughout the central Mediterranean corridor and Britons relocated to the South Pacific were among some the largest migrations to take place during what one historian has labeled the "settler revolution" of the nineteenth century. Whether forced or voluntary, settlerism set in motion a general European diaspora that created new European homelands beyond the continent, in some cases thousands of miles from the mother country.[85]

Outremer Europe was not, however, seen merely as a dumping group for undesirables. Taking a tour of Jamaica in the 1850s on official business for the royal postal service, the novelist Anthony Trollope was enamored by the West Indian planter class which, he believed, embodied all the virtues of his English compatriots. "He has so many of the characteristics of an English country gentleman that he does not strike the Englishman as a strange being," Trollope asserted. The social clubs, balls and "strong old-fashioned local friendships" that existed on the island testified to the authentically Anglo-Saxon qualities found in the colonies.[86] Over the next two decades, Trollope visited and recorded his impressions of several imperial territories ranging from North America to the Pacific. In his writings, he sought to chronicle the experience of a global British community, glorifying the dissemination of the Anglo-Saxon race throughout the world. His books served to introduce Victorian readers to the colonies as they mapped imperial places and reproduced an imperial ideology reinforcing the idea of a greater Anglo-Saxon society beyond the British Isles.[87] By the middle of the nineteenth century, Outremer Europe was becoming a familiar part of a European experience for those with the time and money to travel as well as for the general reading public interested in their nation's overseas colonial territories.

Trollope's imagined Greater Britain was half reality and half fantasy. At the dawn of the 1800s, Maria Nugent, wife of the Jamaican Governor George Nugent, would have hardly agreed with Trollope's encouraging account of the island residents. Rather than gentlemen, their manners were crude and barely "British" by any recognizable standard. The most telling detail was their speech. "The Creole language is not confined to the Negroes," she despaired, complaining of the "broken English" and "indolent drawling" that inflected creole parlance and rendered it unintelligible to a proper English speaker.[88] Similar complaints could be found across the French Antilles where visitors and education reformers warned of the island *patois* and poor French spoken in places such as Guadeloupe and Martinique. "Nowhere does the *patois* reign as despotically as in the colonies," one critic grumbled.[89] Long-term Jamaican resident John Stewart was conscious of the cultural differences that distanced the denizens of the Caribbean Outremer from their compatriots in Britain proper. Slavery had desensitized the creoles to acts of brutality and conditioned certain questionable morals in them. Their tastes and manners remained provincial and shaped by the African influences of the region. Nevertheless, Stewart was optimistic. "The primitive creolian customs and manners are fast disappearing, being superseded by the more polished manners of European life," he admitted in 1823, and this was primarily due to the education that Jamaican children received in the metropole and their greater contact with the motherland.[90] In an age of growing nationalism, integration and education were seen as necessary correctives to the particularism that characterized the Outremer.

Creole localism certainly set Outremer Europe apart from the continent, but it was not the most pronounced difference to be found. Colonists lived surrounded by indigenous peoples. Although colonial settlements were usually designed to segregate the two populations with "European" quarters existing alongside native slums, the separation was far from absolute. The presence of the native imparted a distinct character to colonial societies that was absent on the European continent. In his *Principes des colonisation* published in 1895, the French theorists Arthur Girault put the matter bluntly. "The diversity of races and colors is, in effect, one of the most conspicuous traits of our colonies and at the same time one of the biggest challenges for colonial policy. The difference is striking when compared with the essential homogeneity of France."[91] Given the supposed "homogeneity" of continental nation-states, European identity acquired a particular connotation within the context of the colonies. To be "European" inevitably meant being white, a mark distinguishing settlers from the "diversity of races and colors" that populated the Outremer. Often, as in the case with French Algeria, the varying European nationalities that settled in the region were legally categorized as "European," differentiating them from the indigenous populations by law.[92] European selfhood implied both cultural and racial difference, and the two typically went hand-in-hand as colonization proceeded apace.[93]

However, whiteness and European ancestry was by no means a guarantee of civility in the tropics far from the metropole. As early as the mid-eighteenth century, the French *philosophe* Denis Diderot speculated on the consequences of colonial migration for Europeans, concluding it resulted in the degeneration of national character. The further a traveler resided from their native land, the more diminished was their sense of *"esprit national."* "Once past the equator, a man is neither English, nor Dutch, nor French, nor Spanish, nor Portuguese," he remarked. Colonialism had transformed Europeans into a pack of "savage nomads," a people scattered across a great many countries yet "belonging to none."[94] Most governments expressed fears over national displacement and the loss of identity as Europeans spread out across the globe. States attempted to prevent colonists from "going native" or engaging in any acts that might corrupt their "national character." Laws forbidding inter-racial unions were one such prophylactic, albeit a largely unsuccessful one that proved impossible to enforce. Biological theories on racial purity and degeneration became common within almost all colonial societies, reinforcing the idea of a white and civilized European identity.[95]

Yet even if blood was kept pure and racial identities policed, the colonial milieu itself presented a formidable challenge. A "savage" environment could, theorist posited, exercise a pernicious influence on "civilized" individuals. As one French anthropologist explained, "the milieu of a savage and degraded race can, to a certain degree, take a toll on the civilized man. Habituated to seeing only degenerated beings, he will himself become degraded."[96] Anthropological conjectures raised fundamental questions regarding the status of colonists in relation to their metropolitan counterparts. Planters may have thought of Barbados as "Great Britain in miniature," but many Britons saw reason for doubt. An English visitor to the island in the early-nineteenth century noted that many of the whites on the island had maintained too intimate a contact with African creoles, acquiring their poor manners and habits in the process. This was particularly the case with those who had "not visited Europe nor resided for some time away from the island."[97]

Colonial societies exposed the unique racial and social circumstances differentiating continental Europe from its overseas progenies. Even as public expositions and print culture during the nineteenth century familiarized a greater number of metropolitans with the Outremer, depictions of colonies continued to highlight their exotic and foreign elements. Exhibitions featured African dancers, whirling dervishes and Indian craft workers outfitted in "traditional" dress. Life-sized dioramas of colonial territories contained reconstructions of tapering minarets and thatched huts in a pastiche of Oriental and native influences. These portrayals were often for purposes of entertainment and spectacle, but they endowed imperial territories with foreign attributes that psychologically distanced them from the mother country.[98]

Colonists challenged the Orientalism and primitivism that threatened to set them apart, often stressing their commonalities with fellow compatriots and publishing disquisitions on the cultural and national ties that bound imperial communities together. In 1869, the newspaper *Akhbar* alluded to the "uninterrupted current of people and affairs . . . [and] constant exchange of ideas and sentiments" that united France with the Algerian settler population. "Are there really two countries?" the newspaper asked. "Are they not rather different members of the same body, receiving life and pulsating movements from the same heart?"[99] Colonists in New Zealand expressed a similar view in 1843 vis-à-vis Great Britain, emphasizing patriotism and attachment to the empire as a bond shared with their countrymen. "We are part and parcel of the great British empire. Our sympathy with its glory . . . is not to be extinguished or dimmed by a change of hemisphere or oceans intervening."[100] During the late nineteenth century, Spanish colonial subjects bolstered calls for inclusion under the umbrella of *españolismo*, a cul-

tural nationalist movement asserting a common Spanish heritage
and identity. These claims underpinned demands for empire-wide
citizenship, supporting arguments that the Spanish overseas territories were, in fact, provinces of the crown much like Valencia or
Madrid and should, therefore, be incorporated directly into the body
politic.[101]

Settler communities proved bastions of imperial nationalism and
creole patriotism that transmitted distinct ideas of national identity.
Those at the margins felt compelled to project an image of a global
nationality, if only to establish grounds for inclusion with their metropolitan counterparts. Of course, these sentiments found support
among select metropolitan circles as well. During the 1840s, British
colonial secretary Earl Grey led a colonial reform policy aimed at
extending "the privilege of self-government" and "the dearest rights
of Englishmen" to subjects in Canada and the South Pacific territories. Politicians were not averse to stoking the flames of imperial
patriotism, especially when it permitted an opportunity to demon-
strate their commitment to core British values. Hoping to appeal to
constituents at home, liberals found the white empire an instructive
means of conveying national political ideals of self-sufficiency and
constitutionalism to mass audiences. In the process they encouraged
a vision of a global British community linked through empire and
common values.[102] During the nineteenth century in general, empires effectively became "nationalized." They were used to communicate a wide range of national values and symbols, encouraging

citizens to identify with extended communities beyond national frontiers.[103]

Globalized nationality did not necessarily depend upon formal empire either. Beginning in the late-nineteenth century, Italian sociologists and government officials worried by the exodus of over 12 million metropolitans from the peninsula saw some utility in thinking about Italy as a global nation with emigrant settlements across Europe, North Africa and the Americas. "Greater Italy" became a topic of interest among political elites and led to the creation of an Italian Emigration Commission responsible for liaising and sustaining connections with Italian communities abroad. The politician and economists Luigi Einaudi was keen to promote his vision of a Greater Italy, imagining a constellation of voluntary Italian "colonies" scattered throughout the world yet connected to Italy proper through strong cultural and national ties. "On the banks of the Plata River, a new Italy is rising," he extolled in 1899. "A people is forming which, though Argentine, will preserve the fundamental character of the Italian people and will prove to the world that the imperialist ideal will not remain only an Anglo-Saxon ideal."[104]

The European diaspora provided conditions for imagining expansive communities united through common bonds of *españolismo*, *italianità* or Britishness. Although anxieties over the loss of *"esprit national"* persisted, these anxieties occupied only one theme among many in the rhetoric and discourse of modern European nationalism. Settlers abroad may have looked to the mother country for a source of their identity, but they were hardly passive recipients of ideas emanating from the metropole. Nationalism was not an internally generated concept that was transmitted outward to peripheral regions. The meaning and content of nationality was frequently mediated through and negotiated with co-nationals of the Outremer. During the nineteenth century, colonialism and nationalism came together to inspire different and sometimes conflicting definitions of community. In an age of global empire and resettlement, European nationality itself became a global phenomenon that reverberated across imperial spaces.

———————

"Wear the costume of the country you visit, but keep your own clothes for the journey home," Diderot once advised.[105] This injunction could have served as an epigram for the process of decolonization that was set in motion during the mid-twentieth century. Faced with crippled economies and formidable national resistance movements in the immediate aftermath of the Second World War, Europeans pulled up stakes and retreated back to the continent, either relinquishing formal control over the Outremer or abandoning it altogether. Indeed, it appeared European states endeavored to don a more familiar garb. They abandoned the ornamentation of empire and returned to imagined ancestral homelands, committing themselves to "European integration" and continentalist projects. Yet in the wake of empire, it was difficult to ignore that "home" had changed. Centuries of migration, economic integration and cultural exchange had left their mark on imperial nations, revealing that metropoles had never been divorced from the currents and counterflows of the empires they had founded.[106] Outremer Europe with its racial diversity and heterogeneity had become Europe proper, a realization that elicited new anxieties over *esprit national* and loss of identity in the coming years.

In 1985, the conservative British MP Enoch Powell seemed to be taking a page from the old imperial script when speculating on the growing presence of Africans and Asians in the country. Britain, he warned, would not be "recognizable as the same nation it has been, or perhaps as a nation at all" if immigration trends continued unabated.[107] The verdict has been equally severe among French politicians and conservatives alarmed by an influx of North African immigrants arriving in the country since the postwar period. As one senator remarked during a controversial debate over immigration legislation in 1993, "the majority [of French citizens] do not want a puzzle of cultures, faith and traditions which [will] slowly disfiguring our national identity."[108] The "essential homogeneity" that Arthur Girault attributed to France in the late-nineteenth century had always been a fiction, but this fiction has made the "diversity of races and colors" previously relegated to the colonies a more conspicuous and, some might argue, unwelcome presence in national life.[109] Current anxieties over *esprit national* are a reminder that former colonial powers cannot keep their own clothes for the journey home, not simply because the legacies of empire run deep (although they do), but because imperialism was part of a globalizing process that has yet to run its course.

Until relatively recently, two distinct stories of the European nation were told. One was a "national romance" premised on the development of a collective people coming together through the recognition of common ideals and shared triumphs. This story chronicled the rise of the nation-state, and it is one that continues to be reiterated today in many history books and classrooms. The other story told was that of the "colonial tragedy." *This* story typically emphasized the failure of European nations to make good on their promise to spread "civilization" to other parts of the world and the ignominious collapse of empire that occurred in the wake of the Second World War.

These narratives and plot structures—what Hayden White has called "metahistory"—have not only simplified history. They have served to reinforce certain boundaries central to national memory and have created frameworks for the imagining of a nominally "French" or "British" narrative distinct from the imperial narrative. The "Europeanization" of continental nation-states has required a fair amount of forgetting and even "amnesia," as various critics have noted.[110] National narratives have traditionally treated the imperial experience as a historical tangent, and in doing so marginalized the disparate colonies and multi-ethnic settler communities that once thought of themselves as European despite their distance from an imagined homeland. The Outremer augmented the boundaries and peripheries of Europe in an age characterized by rampant imperialism and global migrations. Colonists in Algiers enjoyed Parisian-style cafés and boulevards reminiscent of Haussmann's Paris just as British residents in Bombay caught trains at the Victoria terminus modeled on London's St. Pancras. These were details in a global European history that was extra-continental but no less European. They provide a view of processes that wove together lives and established connections across great distances, recreating an image of the imperial nation that many subjects and citizens once accepted as a reality. We have only just begun to recover these global narratives. Prior to what scholars have labeled an "imperial turn" in the discipline of history, these details were pegged as histories that occurred "over there." In reconstituting them, we have begun to de-territorialize European memory and, through this, grasp the complex and diverse relations that made up an exceedingly globalized European story.

For more than two centuries, imperialism provided a means of transmitting national identities and values, and in many cases served to strengthen them. Yet in their transmission they often acquired a universality that made them "European" and not just merely national. Imperialism spoke to desires of national grandeur, but it equally promoted them under the guise of "civilization," and that civilization was imagined as one shared among the people of the continent. "Europe has always been open to the entire world," claimed the

Swiss writer and European federalist Denis de Rougemont in 1949. "By right or wrong, by idealism or by ignorance, by virtue of its faith or by its imperialist views, it has always perceived its civilization as an ensemble of universal values."[111] For thinkers of the nineteenth century, this "openness" to the entire world possessed a more evident imperial character, one that was embedded in the very concept of "civilization" Europe embodied. World history, as Hegel pointedly remarked, traveled from East to West, for Europe was "the absolute end of History"— that is to say, modern civilization incarnate.[112] For Hegel, this superior status had come through the torturous struggles of dialectic change and the violent transformation of opposing forces that had propelled European civilization into the modern era.

Arguably, this reading of civilization was a product of a post-revolutionary mentality. It emphasized the destructive and creative impulses and universalism that had shaped the course of the French Revolution as it became a general European revolution. It was through this dramatic rupture with the past and violent act of reformation that a distinct European sense of self was born. If the philosophes spoke of refinement and elevated morals when they invoked civilization, the next generation embellished this concept with new notions of historical discontinuity, radical transformation and freedom that would remain central to the construction of a European master narrative and identity over the next century. Almost from its inception, this vision was channeled into an aggressive project of colonial expansion and overseas transformation that would give Europe a profound sense of its own world-historical significance. The radicalization of the Enlightenment not only inspired faith in the idea that the world could be remade in Europe's image. It rendered it a moral imperative. This process too was "a European tendency" (to employ Mazzini's phrase).

The narrative that has shaped our idea of modern European development amounts to an exercise in dialectics. Only in separating itself completely from its past could Europe create itself anew under the guise of "modern civilization." We may add, moreover, that only through a self-proclaimed world-historical mission could this imaginary be sustained and made real, setting the stage for the era of European imperial expansion that would validate a self-proclaimed modern civilization by pressing it upon others deemed "primitive" and beyond the pale of modernity. It is in this context that we might reflect on what, at present, has been called Europe's "crisis of identity," a phrase encompassing a broad range of debates concerning questions of core values, history, immigration and the impact of globalization.[113] Today, as the attributes of European modernity secure themselves firmly beyond the continent, Europe finds its historic claim to a universal modernizing project compromised. The proliferation of nation-states across former colonial empires, the industrialization of world economies and the establishment of global capitalist markets have relegated Europe to a partner in a larger vision of modernity shared with non-Western societies. Modernity, once seen as a particularly European or Occidental phenomenon, has, in the twenty-first century, acquired its own culture and attributes that can no longer be considered purely Western or European in character.[114] The advent of a postcolonial and globalized modernity entails the end of the European civilizing mission and with it the end of a particular idea of European selfhood and history. At the dawn of the twenty-first century, Europe has lost its monopoly on its universal world-historical status.

We can speculate on whether Europe will exhibit its familiar tendency for radical redefinition and self-recreation. Or we can question whether we need to posit a new European master narrative altogether, resituating its revolutionary and modern heritage as such. The alternative, as some have recently suggested, is to "provincialize" Europe and integrate it into a larger global narrative based upon the recognition of "multiple modernities" and a pluralist history.[115] These questions arrive at a time when European integration and growing demands for multiculturalism have compelled Europeans to reflect critically on questions of identity, nationality and their place in the wider world. Perhaps more to the point, their prevalence suggests that such questions will continue to provide grounds for the affirmation, contestation and reconceptualization of new European imaginaries and narratives in the years ahead.

Notes

[1] Louis Chevalier de Jaucourt, "L'Europe," *Encyclopédie ou Dictionnaire raisonné des sciences, des arts et des métiers*, 36 vols. (Paris: Braisson, 1751-1780), 6:211-12.

[2] Montesquieu, *Pensées et Fragments inédits* (Paris: G. Gounouilhou, 1901), 316.

[3] Quoted in Anthony Pagden, "Introduction," *The Idea of Europe: From Antiquity to the European Union* (Cambridge: Cambridge University Press, 2002), 151.

[4] David Levering Lewis, *God's Crucible: Islam and the Making of Europe, 570-1215* (New York: Norton, 2008), 172.

[5] John Hale, *The Civilization of Europe in the Renaissance* (New York: Atheneum, 1994), 1-50.

[6] Robert Wolker, *Rousseau, The Age of the Enlightenment and Their Legacies* (Princeton: Princeton University Press, 2012), 35-44.

[7] Dena Goodman, *The Republic of Letters: A Cultural History of The French Enlightenment* (Ithaca: Cornell University Press, 1994); David Adams and Galin Tihanov, eds., *Enlightenment Cosmopolitanism* (Oxford: Legenda, 2011); James Van Horn Melton, *The Rise of The Public Sphere in Enlightenment Europe* (Cambridge: Cambridge University Press, 2001).

[8] Anthony Pagden, "Introduction," *The Idea of Europe*, 16.

[9] Adam Smith, *An Inquiry into the Wealth of Nature and Causes of the Wealth of Nations* (London: Metheun, 1961), 1:433.

[10] Quoted in Silvia Sebastiani, *The Scottish Enlightenment: Race, Gender, and the Limits of Progress* (London: Palgrave Macmillan, 2013), 57.

[11] Michael Mosher, "Montesquieu on Empire and Enlightenment," *Empire and Modern Political Thought*, ed., Sankar Muthu (Cambridge: Cambridge University Press, 2012), 151-52.

[12] Sankar Muthu, "Conquest, Commerce and Cosmopolitanism in Enlightenment Political Thought," *Empire and Modern Political Thought*, 204

[13] Stuart Woolf, "The Construction of a European World-View in The Revolutionary-Napoleonic Years," *Past and Present*, 137 (November 1992): 80-81.

[14] Pagden, "Introduction," *The Idea of Europe*, 18-19.

[15] Adam Ferguson, *An Essay on the History of Civil Society* (Edinburgh: Edinburgh University Press, 1966), 1.

[16] Quoted in Brett Bowden, *The Empire of Civilization: The Evolution of an Imperial Idea* (Chicago: University of Chicago Press, 2009), 70.

[17] Wessel Krul, "Volney, Frankenstein and The Lessons of History," *Revolutionary Histories: Transatlantic Cultural Nationalism, 1775-1815*, ed. W. M. Verhoeven (London: Palgrave, 2002), 44.

[18] Quoted in Sebastiani, *The Scottish Enlightenment*, 55.

[19] Jean Antoine Nicolas de Caritat, Marquis de Condorcet, *Sketch for a Historical Picture of the Progress of the Human Mind*, trans., June Barraclough (New York: Noonday, 1955), 177.

[20] Biancamaria Fontana, "The Napoleonic Empire and The European Nations," *The Idea of Europe*, 121-25; Stuart Woolf, *Napoleon's Integration of Europe* (London: Routledge, 1991).

[21] Quoted in Robert Gibson, *Best of Enemies: Anglo-French Relations Since the Norman Conquest* (Exeter: Impress Books, 2004), 157.

[22] Quoted in Stuart Woolf, "French Civilization and Ethnicity in the Napoleonic Empire," *Past and Present*, 124 (August 1989): 114.

[23] Émile Barrault, *Occident et Orient: Études politiques, morales, religieuse* (Paris: A. Pougin, 1835), 253.

[24] Quoted in Maurizio Isabella, "Mazzini's Internationalism in Context: From Cosmopolitan Patriotism of the Italian Carbonari to Mazzini's Europe of the Nations," *Giuseppe Mazzini and The Globalisation of Democratic Nationalism, 1830-1920*, eds., C. A. Bayly and Eugenio F. Biagini (Oxford: Oxford University Press, 2008), 42.

[25] Émile Littré, "Politique," *La Philosophie positive* (Paris: Germer Baillière, 1867), 1:127.

[26] Hale, *The Civilization of the Renaissance*, 15-21.

[27] Mark Bassin, "Russia between Europe and Asia: The Ideological Construction of Geographical Space," *The Slavic Review*, 50 (1991): 6-7.

[28] Kate Brown, *Dispatches From Dystopia: Histories of Places Not Yet Forgotten* (Chicago: University of Chicago Press, 2015), 4.

[29] Denis Diderot, "Observations on the Instruction of the Empress of Russia to the Deputies for the Making of the Laws," *Political Writings*, ed., John Hope Mason and Robert Wokler (Cambridge: Cambridge University Press, 1992), 85.

[30] Louis-Philippe de Ségur, *Memoirs and Reflections*, 3 vols. (London: Henry Colburn, 1827), 2:122.

[31] Quoted in Maria Todorova, *Imagining The Balkans* (New York: Oxford University Press, 1997), 84.

[32] Larry Wolff, *Inventing Eastern Europe: The Map of Civilization on the Mind of the Enlightenment* (Stanford: Stanford University Press, 1994); Ezequiel Adamovsky, "Euro-Orientalism and the Making of the Concept of Eastern Europe in France, 1810-1880," *The Journal of Modern History*, 77 (September 2005): 591-628.

[33] Harry de Windt, *Through Savage Europe* (London: T. Fisher Unwin, 1906).

[34] Quoted in Norman Davies, *Europe: A History* (London: Pimlico, 1997), 55.

[35] Théophile Gautier, *Voyage en Espagne* (Paris: Flammarion, 1981), 263.

[36] Tony Judt, *Postwar: A History of Europe Since 1945* (New York: Penguin, 2005), 752.

[37] William Howard Russell, *My Diary In India In The Year 1858-69*, 2 vols. (London: Routledge, Warne and Routledge, 1860), 1:80-81.

[38] Normand Macleod, *Peeps at The Far East: A Familiar Account of a Visit to India* (London: Strahan, 1871), 25.

[39] Quoted in Tristram Hunt, *Cities of Empire: The British Colonies and the Creation of the Urban World* (New York: Metropolitan Books, 2014), 263.

[40] Rudyard Kipling, *The City of Dreadful Night* (New York: Alex Grosset, 1899), 8.

[41] Henry James, *English Hours*, ed., Alma Louise Lowe (London: William Heinemann, 1960), 42.

[42] Carl E. Schorske, *Fin-de-Siècle Vienna: Politics and Culture* (New York: Vintage, 1980), 24-110.

[43] Letter from Prince Napoleon to the Emperor (undated), *Papiers et Correspondance de la Famille Impériale*, 2 vols. (Paris: Granier Frères, 1871), 1: 381.

[44] Zeynep Çelik, *Urban Forms and Colonial Confrontations: Algiers Under French Rule* (Berkeley: University of California Press, 1997).

[45] Eugene Fromentin, *Between Sea and Sahara: An Algerian Journal* (Athens: Ohio University Press, 1999), 11.

[46] Julia Clancy-Smith, *Mediterraneans: Europe and North Africa in an Age of Migration* (Berkeley: University of California Press, 2012).

[47] Évariste Bavoux, *Alger: Voyage politique et descriptif dans le Nord de l'Afrique*, 2 vols. (Paris: Chez Brockhaus et Avenarius, 1841), 2: 133.

[48] A. de Broglie, *Une Réforme administrative en Afrique* (Paris: H. Dumineray, 1860), 126.

[49] Augustin Marquand, "Alger et ses environs," *Akhbar*, 14 February 1869.

[50] See: Jean Baudrilliard, *Simulacra and Simulation*, trans. Sheila Faria Glaser (Ann Arbor: University of Michigan Press, 1994).

[51] Zeynep Çelik, *Displaying the Orient: Architecture of Islam at Nineteenth-Century World's Fairs* (Berkeley: University of California Press, 1992), 157-58.

[52] Daniel Brower, "Islam and Ethnicity: Russian Colonial Policy in Turkestan," *Russia's Orient: Imperial Borderlands and Peoples, 1700-1917*, eds., Daniel Brower and Edward Lazzerini (Bloomington: Indiana University Press, 1997), 117-20.

[53] Quoted in David Schimmelpenninck van der Oye, *Russian Orientalism: Asia in the Russian Mind from Peter the Great to the Emigration* (New Haven: Yale University Press, 2010), 87.

[54] Henri Morse, *A Trevers l'Asia centrale* (Paris: E. Plon, 1885), 82.

[55] Eugene Schuyler, *Turkistan*, 2 vols. (New York: Scribner and Armstrong, 1877), 1:76-80.

[56] Jeff Sahadeo, *Russian Colonial Society in Tashkent, 1865-1923* (Bloomington: Indiana University Press, 2007), 35-46.

[57] Quoted in Douglas Northrop, *Veiled Empire: Gender and Power in Stalinist Central Asia* (Ithaca: Cornell University Press, 2003), 37.

[58] Quoted in Sahadeo, *Russian Colonial Society in Tashkent*, 44.

[59] See: Alexander Morrison, "Russian Rule in Turkestan and the Example of British India, c. 1860-1917," *The Slavonic and East European Review*, 84:4 (October 2006): 666-707.

[60] Quoted in Xosé-Manoel Núñez, "Nation-Building and Regional Integration: The Case of the Spanish Empire, 1700-1914," *Nationalizing Empires*, eds., Stefan Berger and Alexei Miller (Budapest: Central European University Press, 2015), 236.

[61] Bernard Lewis, *What Went Wrong?: Western Impact and The Middle Eastern Response* (Oxford: Oxford University Press, 2002), 53.

[62] Letter to Louis de Cormenin 5 July 1852, in Théophile Gautier, *Constantinople et autres textes sur la Turquie* (Paris: La Boît à Documents, 1990), 24.

[63] Russell, *My Diary In India*, 1:31.

[64] Çelik, *Displaying the Orient*, 147-51.

[65] Théophile Gautier, *Voyage en Égypte* (Paris: La Boît à Documents, 1991), 38, 75.

[66] Quoted in Robert T. Harrison, *Gladstone's Imperialism in Egypt: Techniques and Domination* (Westport, CT: Greenwood, 1995), 53.

[67] David Wedderburn, "Modern Japan," *The Fortnightly Review*, new series (London: Chapman and Hall, 1878), 23:418.

[68] Cyprian A. G. Bridge, "The City of Kiyôto," *Fraser's Magazine*, new series (London: Longmans Green, 1878), 17: 58.

[69] Ibid., 70.

[70] Ellis Schaap, "Baghdad: Bazaars and Beggars," *The Times of Africa and Oriental Review* (1912 Annual), 22.

[71] Russell, *My Diary In India*, 1:144.

[72] Quoted in Frederick Brown, *Flaubert: A Biography* (New York: Little Brown, 2006), 265.

[73] Ernest Feydeau, *Alger: Étude* (Paris: Editions Bouchene, 2003), 157-58.

[74] Charles Rosher, "Mems of Morocco," *African Times*, 1:12 (June 1913), 376.

75 Fromentin, "Fragments d'un journal de voyage," *Œuvres complètes* (Paris: Galli-mard, 1984), 965.

76 Charls Thierry-Mieg, *Six semaines en Afrique* (Paris: Michel Lévy, 1861), 46.

77 Feydeau, Alger, 149.

78 Eustache-Alexander Carron, *Voyages en Algérie* (Châlons-sur-Marne: Laurent, 1859), 13.

79 Edmund Gibbon Wakefield, *A View on the Art of Colonization* (London: John W. Parker, 1849), 71.

80 Catherine Hall, *Civilizing Subjects: Metropole and Colony in the English Imagination, 1830-1867* (Chicago: University of Chicago Press,2002), 29-33.

81 Jennifer Sessions, *By Sword and Plow: France and the Conquest of Algeria* (Ithaca: Cornell University Press, 2011), 219-249.

82 *Le Moniteur Universel*, 20 September 1848.

83 Michael Heffernan, "The Parisian Poor and the Colonization of Algeria During the Second Republic" *French History*, 3:4 (1989): 377-403; Pamela Pilbeam, *The Saint Simonians in Nineteenth-Century France: From Free Love to Algeria* (New York: Palgrave-Macmillan, 2014), 154-62.

84 Nicholas B. Breyfogle, *Heretics and Colonizers: Forging Russia's Empire in the South Caucasus* (Ithaca: Cornell University Press, 2005).

85 James Bleich, *Replenishing the Earth: The Settler Revolution and the Rise of the Anglo-World* (Oxford: Oxford University Press, 2009); Hall, *Civilizing Subject*, 28-33; Wil-lard Sunderland, *Taming the Wild Field: Colonization and Empire on the Russian Steppe* (Ithaca: Cornell University Press, 2004).

86 Anthony Trollope, *The West Indies and The Spanish Main* (London: Chapman and Hall, 1860), 92.

[87] Catherin Hall, "Going-a-Trolloping: Imperial Man Travels the Empire," *Gender and Imperialism*, ed., Claire Midgley (Manchester: Manchester University Press, 1998), 180-99; John Davidson, "Anthony Trollope and the Colonies," *Victorian Studies*, 12 (March 1969): 305-30; Patrick Brontlinger, *Rule of Darkness: British Literature and Imperialism, 1830-1914* (Ithaca: Cornell University Press, 1988), 4-7.

[88] Frank Cundall, ed., *Lady Nugent's Journal: Jamaica One Hundred Years Ago* (London: Adam and Charles Black, 1907), 132.

[89] Hommaire de Hell, "Coup d'oeil sur la condition de la classes noire dans les colonies françaises des Antilles," *Revue de l'Orient* (1858), 8:258-59.

[90] John Stewart, *A View of The Past and Present State of Jamaica* (Edinburgh: Oliver and Boyd, 1823), 168.

[91] Silyane Larcher, *L'Autre citoyen: L'idéal républicain et les Antilles après l'esclavage* (Paris: Armand Colin, 2014), 203.

[92] Laure Blévis, "Les avatars de la citoyenneté en Algérie colonial ou les paradoxes d'une catégorisation," *Droit et Société*, 48 (2001): 557-580.

[93] Stuart Hall, "The Multi-Cultural Question," *Un/Settled Multiculturalisms: Diasporas, Entanglements, Disruptions*, ed., Barnor Hesse (London: Zed, 2001), 216.

[94] Quoted in Anthony Pagden, "The Effacement of Difference: Colonialism and the Origins of Nationalism in Diderot and Herder," *After Colonialism: Imperial Histories and Postcolonial Displacements*, ed., Gyan Prakash (Princeton: Princeton University Press, 1995), 133-34.

[95] Joyce E. Chaplin, "Race," *The British Atlantic World, 1500-1800*, eds., David Armitage and Michael J. Braddick (Houndsmill: Palgrave Macmillan, 2002), 154-67; Saliha Belmessous, *Assimilation and Empire: Uniformity in French and British Colonies, 1541-1954* (Oxford: Oxford University Press, 2013), 49-53.

[96] M. Bonté, "Résumé analytique des faits produits à l'appui de l'influence des milieu," Séance of 16 July 1863, *Bulletins de la Société d'Anthropologie de Paris* (Paris: Victor Masson, 1863), 4:416.

[97] Quoted in Jerome S. Handler and John T. Pohlmann, "Slave Manumissions and Freedmen in Seventeenth-Century Barbados," *William and Mary Quarterly*, 41:3 (July 1984), 405.

[98] Sandrine Lemaire, Pascal Blanchard and Nicholas Bancel, "Jalons d'une culture colonial sous le Second Empire (1851-1870)," *Culture colonial en France de la Revolution Française à nos jours* (Paris: CNRS Editions, 2008), 99-105; Çelik, *Displaying the Orient*.

[99] *Akhbar*, 13 June 1869.

[100] Alan Lester, "British Settler Discourse and the Circuits of Empire," *History Workshop Journal*, 54 (Autumn 2001), 31.

[101] Josep M. Fradera, "The Empire, the Nation and the Homeland: Nineteenth-Century Spain's National Idea," *Region and State in Nineteenth-Century Europe: Nation-Building, Regional Identities and Separatism*, eds., Joost Augusteijn and Eric Storm (Houndsmill: Palgrave Macmillan, 2012), 141-42.

[102] Jonathan Parry, *The Politics of Patriotism: English Liberalism, National Identity and Europe, 1830-1886* (Cambridge: Cambridge University Press, 2006), 185-90.

[103] Miller and Berger, *Nationalizing Empires*.

[104] Mark I. Choate, *Emigrant Nation: The Making of Italy Abroad* (Cambridge: Harvard University Press, 2008), 51.

[105] Diderot, "The Supplément au Voyage du Bougainville," *Political Writings*, 74.

[106] Frederick Cooper and Ann Laura Stoler, "Between Metropole and Colony: Rethinking a Research Agenda," *Tensions of Empire: Colonial Culture in a Bourgeois*

World, eds., Frederick Cooper and Ann Laura Stoler (Berkeley: University of California Press, 1997), 1-37; Antoinette Burton, ed., *After the Imperial Turn: Thinking with and through the Nation* (Durham: Duke University Press, 2006).

[107] Quoted in Clare E. Alexander, *The Art of Being Black: The Creation of Black British Youth Identities* (Oxford: Clarendon Press, 1996), 5.

[108] Quoted in Soraya Tlatti, "French Nationalism and the Issue of North African Immigration," *Franco-Arab Encounters*, eds., L. Carl Brown and Matthew S. Gordon (Lebanon: American University of Beirut Press, 1996), 393.

[109] Fafid Gafaiti, "Nationalism, Colonialism, and Ethnic Discourse in the Construction of French Identity," *French Civilization and its Discontents: Nationalism, Colonialism, Race*, eds., Tyler Stovall and Georges van den Abbeele (Lanham: Lexington Books, 2003), 189-210.

[110] Benjamin Stora, *La gangrène et l'oubli: la mémoire de la guerre de l'Algérie* (Paris: La Découverte, 2005).

[111] Denis de Rougemont, *Oeuvres complètes*, 3 vols. (Paris: Editions de la Différence, 1994), 1:85.

[112] G. F. W. Hegel, *The Philosophy of History* (New York: Dover, 1956), 103.

[113] Dirk Hoerder, "Transcultural States, Nations and Peoples," *The Historical Practice of Diversity: Transcultural Interactions From the Early Modern Mediterranean to the Postcolonial World*, ed., Dirk Hoerder (New York: Berghan, 2003), 26-29; Nezar Alsayyad, "Muslim Europe ort Euro-Islam: On the Discourses of Identity and Culture," *Muslim Europe or Euro-Islam: Politics, Culture and Civilization in the Age of Globalization*, eds., Nezar Alsayyad and Manuel Castelles (Lanham: Lexington Book, 2002), 9-30; Anthony Giddens, *Run-Away World: How Globalization is Reshaping Our Lives* (London: Routledge, 2003); Crawford Young, ed., *The Rising Tide of Cultural Pluralism:*

The Nation-State at Bay? (Madison: University of Wisconsin Press, 1993); Sharon MacDonald, *Memorylands: Heritage and Identity in Europe Today* (London: Routledge, 2013).

[114] Carol Gluck, "The End of Elsewhere: Writing Modernity Now," *The American Historical Review*, 116:2 (June 2011): 677-79; Hichem Djaït, *Europe and Islam*, trans., Peter Heinegg (Berkeley: University of California Press, 1985), 166-67.

[115] Dipesh Chakrabarty, *Provincializing Europe: Postcolonial Thought and Historical Difference* (Princeton: Princeton University Press, 2000); Eisenstadt, "Multiple Modernities," *Daedalus*,129:1 (2000): 1-29; Huri İslamoğlu and Peter C. Perdue, "Introduction," in *Shared Histories of Modernity: China, India and The Ottoman Empire*, ed., Huri İslamoğlu and Peter C. Perdue (New Delhi: Routledge, 2009), 1-20.

www.ingramcontent.com/pod-product-compliance
Lightning Source LLC
Chambersburg PA
CBHW032121280326
41933CB00009B/934